Contents

KU-145-167

Some words are shown in bold, **like this**. You can find out what they mean by looking in the Glossary.

What is physical activity?

Physical activity is any activity that burns energy through movement. Playing catch, walking, and climbing playground equipment are all physical activities. Some types of physical activity are **unstructured.** They are not scheduled or planned out. Building a snowman, running up the stairs, and cycling are all forms of unstructured physical activity.

Exercise is **structured** physical activity. It is scheduled and organized. Going for a 1.6-kilometre (one-mile) run five days a week is exercise. Doing 50 sit-ups every morning or attending a swimming class three times a week are forms of exercise.

Unstructured activities suc as skateboar can be a lot of fun.

NEWSFLASH

Children and teenagers are becoming more inactive. They often ride in cars rather than walk or ride bikes. The average child in Britain spends 25 hours per week watching television. They also play video games and surf the Internet instead of playing outdoors. Children who spend more time outdoors are more physically active.

613.71

...DEAL

g Fit

BNBC MN

Please return/renew this item by the last date shown.

To renew this item, call **0845 0020777** (automated)
or visit **www.librarieswest.org.uk**

Borrower number and PIN required.

Libraries West

-Jan-2009

.99

een

Heinemann

1 9 0017292 9

www.heinemann.co.uk/library
Visit our website to find out more information about Heinemann Library books.

To order:

 Phone 44 (0) 1865 888112

 Send a fax to 44 (0) 1865 314091

Visit the Heinemann bookshop at www.heinemann.co.uk/library to browse our catalogue and order online.

First published in Great Britain by Heinemann Library, Halley Court, Jordan Hill, Oxford OX2 8EJ, part of Pearson Education.

Heinemann is a registered trademark of Pearson Education Ltd.

© Pearson Education Ltd 2008
First published in paperback in 2009
The moral right of the proprietor has been asserted.

All rights reserved. No part of this publication may be reproduced, stored in a retrieval system, or transmitted in any form or by any means, electronic, mechanical, photocopying, recording, or otherwise, without either the prior written permission of the publishers or a licence permitting restricted copying in the United Kingdom issued by the Copyright Licensing Agency Ltd, 90 Tottenham Court Road, London W1T 4LP (www.cla.co.uk).

Editorial: Nancy Dickmann
Design: Richard Parker and Tinstar Design Ltd
Illustrations: Darren Lingard
Picture Research: Mica Brancic and Frances Topp
Production: Alison Parsons

Originated by Chroma Graphics
Printed and bound in China by Leo Paper Group

ISBN 978 0 431 90731 4 (hardback)
12 11 10 09 08

10 9 8 7 6 5 4 3 2 1

ISBN 978 0 431 90738 3 (paperback)
13 12 11 10 09

10 9 8 7 6 5 4 3 2 1

British Library Cataloguing in Publication Data
Sheen, Barbara.
  Keeping fit. - (The real deal)
1. Exercise - Physiological aspects - Juvenile literature
2. Physical fitness - Juvenile literature
I. Title
613.7'1

A full catalogue record for this book is available from the British Library.

Acknowledgments
The publishers would like to thank the following for permission to reproduce photographs:
Alamy pp. **4** (Mary-Ella Keith), **6** (Elvele Images/Alexandra Carlile); Corbis pp. **8** (Simon Marcus), **12** (Duomo), **17** (ImageShop), **18** (Zefa/Anna Peisl), **22** (Mike Watson Images); Getty Images pp. **5** (Taxi/Michael Heinsen), **7** (Taxi/Chris Clinton), **10** (Taxi/Erik Dreyer), **13** (Photonica/Johannes Kroemer), **19** (Taxi/Stephanie Rausser), **23** (Taxi/Tony Anderson), **25** (Taxi/Hans Neleman), **27** (Neo Vision); Jupiter/Botanica/Tanya Constantine p. **11**; Masterfile pp. **21** (Peter Griffith); Photolibrary.com/Image 100 p. **26**; Reuters/Action Images/Adrees Latif p. **15**; SuperStock pp. **9** (age fotostock), **20** (Anton Vengo).

Cover photograph of an arrow road sign reproduced with permission of iStockphoto/Nicholas Belton; photographs of a baseball player jumping and a young girl jogging reproduced with permission of Corbis.

The publishers would like to thank Philip Smith for his assistance in the preparation of this book.

Every effort has been made to contact copyright holders of any material reproduced in this book. Any omissions will be rectified in subsequent printings if notice is given to the publishers.

Disclaimer
All the Internet addresses (URLs) given in this book were valid at the time of going to press. However, due to the dynamic nature of the Internet, some addresses may have changed, or sites may have changed or ceased to exist since publication. While the author and publishers regret any inconvenience this may cause readers, no responsibility for any such changes can be accepted by either the author or the publishers.

It is recommended that adults supervise children on the Internet.

Top Tips

Being healthy is not just about being active. Diet is also important to good health. People should drink at least eight glasses of water a day. The human body is about 60 percent water. It cannot function without water. Getting eight to ten hours of sleep a night is also important, especially while you are growing.

Exercise strengthens a football player's body.

All physical activity is good for the body. It uses the muscles and joints and strengthens the body. It improves our health and burns energy. It even makes us feel good.

Why be active?

People are physically active for many reasons. Being active is fun. It is an important part of living. Some people have a goal. They may be trying to improve their health or the way they look. They may be trying to get in better shape or develop a specific skill so they can be better at a sport. People should be active every day.

How to keep fit

Everyone needs to take responsibility for staying healthy. This responsibility includes being active. Different kinds of physical activity have different effects on the body. There are three main types of physical activities. Try to do a mix of all three types.

Breathing hard

Aerobic activity is one type of physical activity. Running, cycling, skating, swimming, and dancing are some aerobic activities. Aerobic activity makes you breathe harder and increases your **heart rate.** It makes the heart beat faster and strengthens it. A strong heart can pump blood easily.

Swimming for at least 20 minutes strengthens the heart and lungs.

NEWSFLASH

Physical activity develops **motor skills**. These are the skills that help a person move easily. Running, hopping, kicking, jumping, catching, throwing, and skipping are basic motor skills. Developing a wide range of motor skills makes it easier for people to learn specific skills needed for sports.

Top Tip

Lifting weights is a popular strengthening activity, but it is not for children. A child's bones are still developing, and weight lifting can hurt them. Using the resistance of your own body is safer.

Using the resistance of the body is a safe way to gain strength.

Getting stronger

Strengthening activity (also called **anaerobic activity**) makes the muscles stronger. Having strong muscles makes it easier to lift things and move. Strengthening activities work the muscles against an opposing force or **resistance.** For example, a pull-up works the muscles in a person's arms, back, and shoulders against the resistance of the body itself.

Strengthening activities usually involve short bursts of activity. They often make the muscles tired, but do not necessarily leave you out of breath. Sit-ups, pull-ups, and push-ups are strengthening activities. So are martial arts, gymnastics, and climbing.

Stretching out

Flexibility activities stretch the muscles. They help improve movement and balance. Stretching, dancing, and yoga are a few activities that build flexibility.

Martial arts such as tai chi increase strength, balance, and flexibility.

Levels of physical activity

The **intensity,** or level, of each of the three kinds of physical activity can vary. Light physical activity uses twice the energy of resting. It makes the heart rate go up slightly. Walking slowly is an example of a light physical activity.

Moderate physical activity uses three to six times more energy than resting. It causes an increase in breathing and heart rate. Walking briskly, cycling on a flat surface, and bowling are moderate physical activities.

Vigorous physical activity is the hardest. It gets the heart pounding. It makes you feel warm. It uses seven or more times the energy of resting. Running, skipping, swimming laps, and cycling uphill are examples of vigorous physical activities.

Which is best?

All three levels of physical activity are valuable. Levels may vary from one person to another. For example, running 1,500 metres (one mile) may be a moderate physical activity for a top athlete. Walking 1,500 metres may be moderate exercise for a person of average fitness. People who are not very fit should start any exercise program with light physical activity. As they get fitter, they can progress to more vigorous activity.

Top Tip

How much physical activity do you get? To answer this question, think about the word FITT. FITT stands for:

- Frequency (how often you are active)
- Intensity (how hard you work)
- Time (how long you are active)
- Type (what kind of activity you do)

Keeping FITT in mind will help keep you fit!

To prevent injury, start lightly when trying a new type of activity. Moderate activity is best in hot weather. Exercising vigorously in the heat can lead to heatstroke, a serious condition where the body cannot cool itself down.

Walking briskly is a moderate-level physical activity.

Getting it right

Staying active is healthy and fun. But be careful not to overdo physical activities. Children and teenagers should do moderate to vigorous physical activity for at least 60 minutes each day. This does not have to be done all at once. Being active for ten minutes at a time six times a day also counts.

The type of activity also affects the time a person should spend doing it. For example, to get the most benefit for the heart, aerobic activities should last at least 20 minutes. Anaerobic activity can be done for shorter periods. Activities such as walking to school, playing sports, or washing a car count towards the 60-minute target.

Warming up before a game helps prevent injuries.

Cooling down keeps muscles from feeling sore.

Warming up and cooling down

Overdoing physical activity or doing an activity that is too hard can cause injuries. If a person feels pain during physical activity, it means that he or she is pushing the body too far.

A **warm-up** and **cool down** help prevent injuries. Warming up for five minutes before a physical activity loosens and warms the muscles. It gets the body ready to work by slowly raising the heart rate.

Cooling down by stretching for five minutes at the end of a workout gradually lowers the heart rate. It keeps muscles from being stiff and sore. It relaxes the body.

Top Tip

During moderate or vigorous aerobic activity, taking the talk test helps you tell if you are exercising at a healthy level. If you are gasping for breath, your heart is working too hard. If you can sing a song, your heart is not working hard enough. If you can talk without panting, the level is just right.

Keeping it safe

Ignoring safety issues can cause injuries. Although you do not need to buy a whole new wardrobe, it is important to wear the right clothing for certain physical activities. Trainers keep a person from slipping and falling. Socks cushion the feet. Wearing a hat and gloves for playing in the snow, skiing, or ice-skating prevents frostbite. In hot weather, loose fitting shirts and shorts keep the body cool.

For some activities, using safety gear is vital. Wearing a bike helmet or shin guards can make the difference between having fun and getting hurt.

What do you think?

Should there be a law requiring bicycle riders to wear helmets? Some countries have this law while others do not. Those in favour believe that helmets protect people from head injuries. Those against the law believe that wearing a helmet should be a personal choice. They say that when helmets are required, fewer people ride bikes.

Safety gear protects an in-line skater.

During a game, athletes should drink 100ml (about half a cup) of water every 15 minutes.

Eating right

Food provides energy for physical activity. Everyone needs a variety of foods that are rich in **nutrients.** Nutrients are substances in food that keep the body working. Protein, carbohydrates, vitamins, minerals, fats, and water are the nutrients we need. People who get enough nutrients are stronger, more alert, and less likely to be injured during physical activity.

In particular, complex carbohydrates such as beans, nuts, and whole grains give the body long-lasting energy. Many athletes eat them before an event.

Drinking plenty of water is important too. Physical activity can make people overheat or sweat. If they do not replace the water they lose, they can become **dehydrated.** This means the body does not have enough water to work properly. Being dehydrated makes people sick. Stopping to drink water before, during, and after physical activity prevents dehydration.

A strong body

Physical activity strengthens the bones, joints, and muscles of the body. Bones are the frame that holds up the body. The stronger and thicker they are, the less likely they are to break. **Weight-bearing activities** are activities that people do on their feet. They strengthen the bones. Walking and running and sports such as basketball, lacrosse, and tennis are just a few weight-bearing activities.

Physical activities that improve flexibility strengthen the joints. They become easier to bend, rotate, and extend. This helps prevent injury to the muscles surrounding the joints.

What do you think?

The government recommends that schools provide at least two hours of physical education every week. They say it keeps students healthier. It prevents them from becoming **obese**. Some people say that physical education uses up time that should be used for academic subjects. Do you think schools should be required to have physical education classes?

Muscles and bones give the body shape and allow it to move.

Strong bones and muscles helped these Olympic marathon champions win.

Top Tip

Adult athletes may have large, bulging muscles. Adults, especially adult males, produce a chemical called testosterone that makes this possible. Children do not. Before puberty, the body cannot build large, bulging muscles. Puberty is the time in life when a child's body develops into that of an adult.

Muscles

Our muscles do everything from keeping the blood flowing to making it possible for the body to move. Muscles are attached to the body's bones. Physical activity makes the muscles stronger and more flexible. Strengthening the muscles improves **endurance,** or staying power. Strong, flexible muscles are less likely to tear than weak muscles. They allow the body to work and play harder and longer.

Together, strong muscles, bones, and joints help the body. They reduce the risk of injury. They allow the body to move easily and give it better balance. They also improve **posture.**

The heart

The heart is one of the body's most important muscles. It can be strengthened through aerobic physical activity. The heart's job is to pump blood rich in **oxygen** to the rest of the body.

All the parts of the body need oxygen in order to work. The harder the body works, the more oxygen it needs. During physical activity the lungs have to draw in more oxygen. The heart has to pump faster to move oxygen from the lungs to the body. That is why the heart may beat twice as fast during physical activity as it does when the body is at rest.

Top Tip

Using a pedometer can help you check how active you are. A pedometer clips on to your waistband and counts how many steps you take. Two thousand steps is 1.6 kilometres (one mile). The recommendation is to take 10,000 steps a day. The pedometer lets you know if you reached this goal.

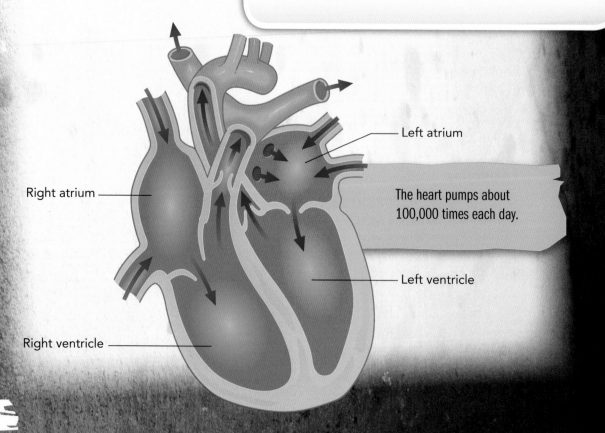

Right atrium

Left atrium

The heart pumps about 100,000 times each day.

Left ventricle

Right ventricle

Top Tip

Measure your heart rate during aerobic activities by pressing your index finger on the side of your wrist for 10 seconds. Count the number of beats you feel, then multiply by six. This is your heart rate. An eight- to eleven-year-old child's target heart rate while exercising should be about 130.

Being physically active can help people live longer.

Exercising the heart

Regular physical activity forces the heart and lungs to work together more effectively. It helps improve breathing capacity as each breath takes in more air. It makes the heart a stronger, better pump. A strong heart does not have to work as hard. It pumps more blood with each beat than a weak heart.

People with strong hearts are less likely to get heart disease or have high blood pressure. Both conditions can cause serious health problems. Heart disease is the leading cause of death in the United Kingdom.

After sitting in school all day, it is fun to be active.

Burning energy

Another way physical activity keeps people healthy is by burning energy in the form of joules (kJ) or **calories** (kcal). These units measure the amount of energy in food. If a person takes in more energy than the body needs, the extra energy is stored as fat. Excess fat can make a person overweight or obese.

Overweight people carry more body fat than is healthy. Obese people are more than 20 percent above their normal body weight. Overweight and obese people are more likely to get heart disease, cancer, diabetes, high blood pressure, and arthritis than other people. Some researchers say that being overweight or obese can shorten a person's life by as much as five years.

What do you think?

More children are becoming overweight. Some people say that school children should be weighed, and parents told if their child is overweight. Some people say this could make children feel different, and that the government should not interfere in people's lives like this.

Burning extra energy

Physical activity helps keep people from becoming overweight. Physical activity does not just burn energy while people are active. It can also raise the amount of energy the body uses for up to 48 hours. Depending on the person, the body may burn anywhere from 40 to 630 extra kJ in the hours following physical activity. For people who are active every day, that adds up to 280 to 4,400 kJ a week.

Top Tip

In 30 minutes, a 45 kilogram (7-stone) person burns about the following number of kJ:

Stretching, playing catch	250 kJ
Playing Frisbee, miniature golf	300 kJ
Playing rounders	500 kJ
Climbing hills, ice-skating, playing football	700 kJ
Playing hockey, tag rugby, basketball, lacrosse, doing sit-ups or push-ups	800 kJ
Martial arts, skipping	1000 kJ

Physical activity such as jumping on a trampoline burns energy and helps prevent obesity.

A happy, healthy lifestyle

Physical activity not only improves physical health, but it is also good for mental health. It makes life more pleasant. It promotes confidence, helps people connect with others, and builds character.

Say good-bye to stress

Physical activity helps reduce **stress.** Stress is a condition that affects people mentally and physically. All kinds of things cause stress. Moving to a new home, problems with friends and family, and taking tests are just a few stressful situations.

Stress is not healthy. It causes muscles to tense. It raises the body's blood pressure and heart rate. This can make a person feel nervous and jittery. Stress can also make a person feel troubled, upset, or sad. It causes people to lose sleep. It can lead to heart problems and asthma attacks. It weakens the body's ability to fight disease.

Trying to keep up with schoolwork can cause stress.

Case Study

Teenager Catrin was under a lot of stress. She heard that exercise could help. She was not physically active, but she decided to try it. She went to a community centre, where she walked on a treadmill three days a week. It helped. Catrin felt calmer after every walk.

Yoga is a relaxing activity that reduces stress.

Be active and relax

Moderate to vigorous physical activity makes the brain release natural chemicals called **endorphins** and **serotonin.** These chemicals reduce stress. They give people a feeling of wellbeing. They improve a person's mood. This is one reason people feel good after they exercise. These good feelings can last up to two hours after the physical activity is over.

Physical activity also relaxes tense muscles. It helps people sleep better. It helps people under stress fight illnesses such as colds and flu. Studies have shown that people who are regularly physically active are less likely to get sick after a stressful situation.

Building confidence

Physical activity can improve **self-confidence.** When people are self-confident, they feel good about themselves. They believe in themselves and their abilities.

Physically active people often set personal goals for themselves. Not everyone's goals are the same. They depend on each person's fitness level. One person's goal may be as simple as taking a walk every night after dinner. Another's can be as challenging as setting a record at an athletics event.

Reaching physical goals helps people discover what they are capable of achieving. This makes people feel more in control, and more likely to try new things.

Meeting personal goals takes mental and physical strength.

NEWSFLASH

Does physical activity raise intelligence? Researchers tested this theory on a group of active and inactive mice. Both groups were put in a maze. The active mice did better at solving the maze. They also had twice as many new brain cells as the inactive mice. Being active appeared to cause the brain cells to grow.

Having self-confidence makes meeting new people easier.

Peer pressure

Being self-confident helps in social situations. Self-confident people are less afraid to talk to new people. Self-confidence helps people deal with **peer pressure.** Peer pressure is pressure put on a person by others to behave in a certain way.

It is normal to want to fit in. Even self-confident people may give in to peer pressure sometimes. But because self-confident people feel good about themselves, they are less likely to think they will be rejected if they do not give in to peer pressure.

Top Tip

In an effort to be stronger and look more muscular, some athletes use **steroids**. This is a bad idea. Steroids are dangerous, illegal drugs. They can be addictive. They cause acne, and can cause liver cancer and heart attacks. They can shorten a person's life.

Building character

Physical activity teaches people about **perseverance** and **cooperation.** Setting goals and working toward them, without giving up, builds perseverance. People with perseverance are likely to finish what they start no matter how hard the job. Perseverance helps people to succeed at work and school.

Teamwork

Physical activities that involve others take cooperation. Team sports require cooperation. For example, in a basketball game, players must work as a team to score. Being able to cooperate helps people get along better with others.

Playing on a sports team also brings people together. Although team members may start out as strangers, working and having fun together makes them closer. Sharing a common goal helps team members to bond.

Being active together is a healthy way for families to get to know each other better.

Sharing a common interest helps people make friends.

Making friends

Physical activity and exercise can help people make friends. It is easier to meet and talk to new people when you share a common interest. Under normal circumstances, people might feel uncomfortable talking to someone they do not know. But, if people meet in dance class, or on a football pitch, or in a skate park, it is natural to talk to each other. Their common interest gives them a reason to want to get to know each other.

Top Tip

Physical activity can help bring families closer together. Many families make fitness a part of their lives. Going bike riding with your parents or fishing with your granddad, for example, are fun and healthy ways to spend time together. Some families go on holidays where they hike, ski, camp, or snorkel as a group.

Having fun

There are a lot of great ways to be physically active. Organized or unorganized group activities are a fun way to be physically active. Team sports such as hockey, football, basketball, and netball, as well as exercise and dance classes are all organized group activities. Some people form clubs, such as a walking club, so they can do their favourite activity with others. Other group activities such as playing tag are less organized, but are still fun.

Pair and solo activities

Some activities such as tennis, ping-pong, and one-on-one basketball take two people. Other activities give us a chance to be alone. Walking, swimming, running, kayaking, and kite flying all can be solo activities. They can also be done with others.

Some physical activities such as horseback riding involve animals. Playing fetch or walking or jogging with a dog is fun too.

Kite flying can be a fun group activity.

Dogs make great walking companions.

More fun

Some activities, such as tug-of-war and martial arts, test a person's strength. Swimming, diving, water polo, body boarding, surfing, snorkelling, water skiing, and rowing give people a chance to have fun in the water. Skiing allows people to enjoy the snow, as does building snow forts, making snow angels, and sledging. In-line skating, skateboarding, and cycling make people active on wheels. Dancing, whether its tap, hip-hop, folk, or ballet, gets people moving to music.

One thing is certain: there is no better way to have fun and keep fit than through physical activity.

Top Tips

Group, pair, and solo activities are all more fun when you do not get hurt. No matter what the activity, warming up and cooling down always help prevent injuries. Good warm-up activities include fast walking and stretches such as side bends, knee lifts, and calf stretches. Good cool-down activities include slow walking, sitting toe-touch, arm and shoulder stretches, and thigh stretches.

Stretching chart

You should stretch your muscles as part of your regular warm-up. Stretching is also great as a cool down activity. Here are some simple stretches to get you started. Remember:

- Make sure you have warmed up a little first. This can be as simple as jogging for a while.
- Hold each stretch for 10–20 seconds.
- Breathe steadily while you stretch slowly.
- Stretch only until the muscle feels tight. If it hurts, you are stretching too far.
- Try to stretch for about 15 minutes.

Lace your fingers together. Turn your arms "inside out," then pull up and stretch. This stretches your arms, shoulders, and your upper back.

Put one hand on your elbow and pull arm across your chest. Repeat with the other arm. This stretches your shoulders and back.

Sit down with your legs out in front of you. Bend one leg so the bottom of your foot touches the thigh of your other leg. Bend forward slightly. This stretches your hamstrings.

Lie on your back and pull your knee to your chest. Repeat with the other leg. This stretches your back.

Step forward with one leg and bend your knee. Put your hands on your knee for balance. This stretches your calf.

Activity level chart

Getting active is both easy and fun. Here are some suggestions for moderate and vigorous activities to try.

Moderate Activity	Vigorous Activity
Walking at a moderate pace on a flat surface, such as walking the dog or walking to school	Running or jogging
Hiking	Climbing briskly up a hill
In-line skating at a moderate speed	Backpacking
Cycling on a fairly flat surface, at a moderate speed	In-line skating at a brisk pace
Yoga	Cycling quickly or on hilly terrain
Jumping on a trampoline	Martial arts (karate, judo, tae kwon do)
Playing tennis (doubles)	Skipping
Playing rounders	Playing tennis (singles)
Shooting baskets	Playing rugby
Playing catch	Playing football
Playing badminton	Playing basketball
Ice-skating at a moderate pace	Playing tennis
Snorkelling or swimming for fun	Ice-skating at a brisk pace
Playing hopscotch or dodgeball	Sledding, tobogganing, or cross-country skiing
Skateboarding	Playing ice hockey
Raking leaves, gardening, or shovelling light snow	Swimming laps
	Shovelling heavy snow

Glossary

aerobic activity sustained physical activity that requires oxygen

anaerobic activity physical activity that does not need oxygen. It uses fuel already stored in the muscles.

calorie measure of the amount of energy in food

cool down light activity at the end of vigorous or moderate physical activity

cooperation working and getting along with others

dehydrated not having enough water in the body

endorphin chemical released by the brain during physical activity that produces a feeling of wellbeing

endurance the ability to do something over a period of time

exercise structured physical activity

flexibility moving joints such as the knee, elbow, ankle, or shoulder through their range of motion

heart rate number of times the heart beats each minute

intensity strength, power, or force of an activity; level

motor skill ability to use muscles effectively for movement

nutrient substance in food that helps the body to grow and function

obese being more than 20 percent above normal body weight

oxygen gas that is essential for life

peer pressure social pressure to behave or look a certain way in order to be accepted by a group

perseverance determination to continue with a task, no matter how difficult it is

physical activity any activity that burns energy through movement

posture way a person carries his or her body

resistance opposing force

self-confidence belief in one's abilities

serotonin chemical released by the brain during physical activity that produces a feeling of wellbeing

steroid substance that encourages muscle growth

stress emotional pressure

structured organized or planned

unstructured not organized or planned

warm-up light physical activities that prepare the body for moderate or vigorous activities

weight-bearing activity activity in which people are upright and carry their own body weight

Further resources

Books

Fit: Clue-up, Wise-Up, Shape-Up!, Lisa Regan (Miles Kelly Publishing, 2005)

Keeping Fit (Healthy Kids), Sylvia Goulding (Cherrytree Books, 2006)

Wise Guide: Fit, Anita Naik (Hodder & Stoughton, 2005)

Websites

BBC Learning: Sport and Fitness
http://www.bbc.co.uk/learning/subjects/sports_and_fitness.shtml

Our Kids Sports
http://www.ourkidsports.com/

Superkids
http://www.super-kids.com/sports.html

Youth Sport Trust
http://www.youthsporttrust.org/

Australian Sports Commission
http://www.ausport.gov.au

Organizations

Sport England
3rd Floor Victoria House
Bloomsbury Square
London WC1B 4SE
Tel: 08458 508 508 (Monday – Friday 8am to 6pm)
Fax: 020 7383 5740
E-mail: info@sportengland.org
Web: http://www.sportengland.org/

British Heart Foundation
14, Fitzhardinge Street
London, W1H 6DH.
Tel: 020 7935 0185
Web: http://www.bhf.org.uk

Index